INVASIVE SPECIES

KUDZU

by Alicia Z. Klepeis

Ideas for Parents and Teachers

Pogo Books let children practice reading informational text while introducing them to nonfiction features such as headings, labels, sidebars, maps, and diagrams, as well as a table of contents, glossary, and index.

Carefully leveled text with a strong photo match offers early fluent readers the support they need to succeed.

Before Reading

- "Walk" through the book and point out the various nonfiction features. Ask the student what purpose each feature serves.
- Look at the glossary together. Read and discuss the words.

Read the Book

- Have the child read the book independently.
- Invite him or her to list questions that arise from reading.

After Reading

- Discuss the child's questions. Talk about how he or she might find answers to those questions.
- Prompt the child to think more. Ask: Scientists study how climate change affects kudzu. Do you think climate change might help kudzu spread? Why or why not?

Pogo Books are published by Jump!
5357 Penn Avenue South
Minneapolis, MN 55419
www.jumplibrary.com

Library of Congress Cataloging-in-Publication Data

Names: Klepeis, Alicia, 1971- author.
Title: Kudzu / by Alicia Z. Klepeis.
Description: Minneapolis, MN: Jump!, Inc., [2023]
Series: Invasive species | Includes index.
Audience: Ages 7-10
Identifiers: LCCN 2022023613 (print)
LCCN 2022023614 (ebook)
ISBN 9798885241106 (hardcover)
ISBN 9798885241113 (paperback)
ISBN 9798885241120 (ebook)
Subjects: LCSH: Kudzu–Juvenile literature.
Invasive plants–Juvenile literature.
Classification: LCC QK495.L52 K54 2023 (print)
LCC QK495.L52 (ebook)
DDC 583/.63–dc23/eng/20220608
LC record available at https://lccn.loc.gov/2022023613
LC ebook record available at https://lccn.loc.gov/2022023614

Editor: Eliza Leahy
Designer: Emma Bersie

Photo Credits: F_studio/Shutterstock, cover; Keithspaulding/Dreamstime, 1; Doikanoy/Shutterstock, 3, 5 (seed pods); Kazu Inoue/Shutterstock, 4, 10-11; russting/Shutterstock, 5 (flower); Cavan Images/Alamy, 6-7; igaguri_1/iStock, 8; National Archives and Records Administration, 9; J.K. York/Shutterstock, 12-13; Bob Pool/Shutterstock, 14-15 (left); TonyLMoorePhoto/iStock, 14-15 (right); JIANG HONGYAN/Shutterstock, 16; tawanroong/Shutterstock, 17; Used with permission of the Alabama Cooperative Extension System (Alabama A&M University and Auburn University). All rights to the original material are reserved by the Alabama Cooperative Extension System. More information is provided at www.aces.edu, 18-19; Chris Landsberger/The Oklahoman/AP Images, 20-21; helloseed/Shutterstock, 23.

Printed in the United States of America at Corporate Graphics in North Mankato, Minnesota.

TABLE OF CONTENTS

CHAPTER 1

ONE SPEEDY VINE

What plant can grow one foot (0.3 meters) in a day? This fast-growing **vine** is kudzu!

flower

seed pods

Kudzu flowers are usually purple or red. They smell like grapes! Insects are drawn to the scent. Honeybees and butterflies **pollinate** kudzu. This makes it possible for seeds to grow.

Kudzu is a weed. It grows where people do not want it to. It **adapts** well and lives in many **habitats**. It grows in forests and fields and on steep hills. It can even cover buildings! It can survive long periods without water.

This plant is **native** to eastern Asia. It is an **invasive species** in many countries. This includes the United States.

TAKE A LOOK!

Where has kudzu been found in the United States? Take a look!

UNITED STATES

ATLANTIC OCEAN

PACIFIC OCEAN

GULF OF MEXICO

1

2 HAWAII

■ = Kudzu invasive range

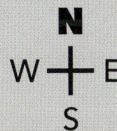

N
W E
S

CHAPTER 2

HARMING HABITATS

The Japanese government sent kudzu to the United States in 1876. It was sent for a special **exhibit**. People saw it. They enjoyed its beautiful flowers and scent. They wanted to plant it in their gardens.

The U.S. government urged farmers to plant kudzu from the 1930s to 1950s. Why? They hoped it would help prevent **erosion**. More than 1 million acres (404,686 hectares) were planted! This helped it spread.

Kudzu can grow sideways. **Runners** spread across the ground. Roots form at their **nodes**. Then, new kudzu plants grow. Kudzu also spreads by underground runners called **rhizomes**.

runner

tree

Kudzu's big leaves block sunlight from reaching native plants and trees. It also takes **nutrients** and water from the soil. This leads to less **biodiversity**.

The plant also harms animals. How? It takes away food from animals that eat native plants.

Kudzu can make railroad tracks slippery. This is dangerous for trains. People must remove the plant from the tracks.

They remove it from power lines, too. The plant can grow into wires. This can cause power losses. Kudzu damage costs the United States more than $100 million each year.

DID YOU KNOW?

Parks lose money due to kudzu. Why? Fewer people visit areas that have been taken over by the weed.

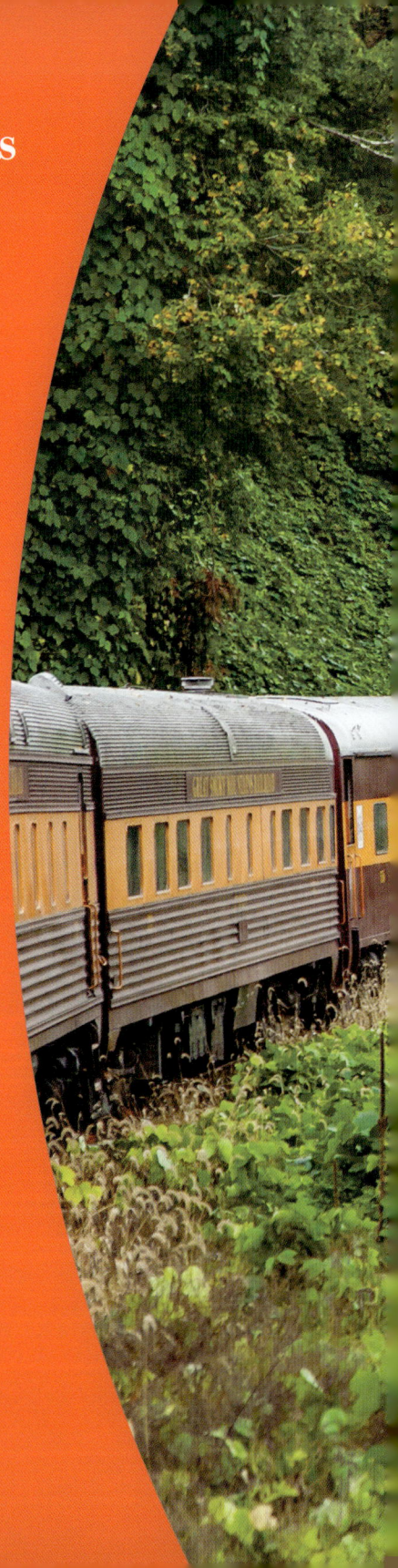

CHAPTER 3

KNOCKING OUT THE WEED

In Asia, kudzu is not a problem. Why? Many insects eat it. People use its roots for medicine. They make food and clothes out of it.

kudzu root

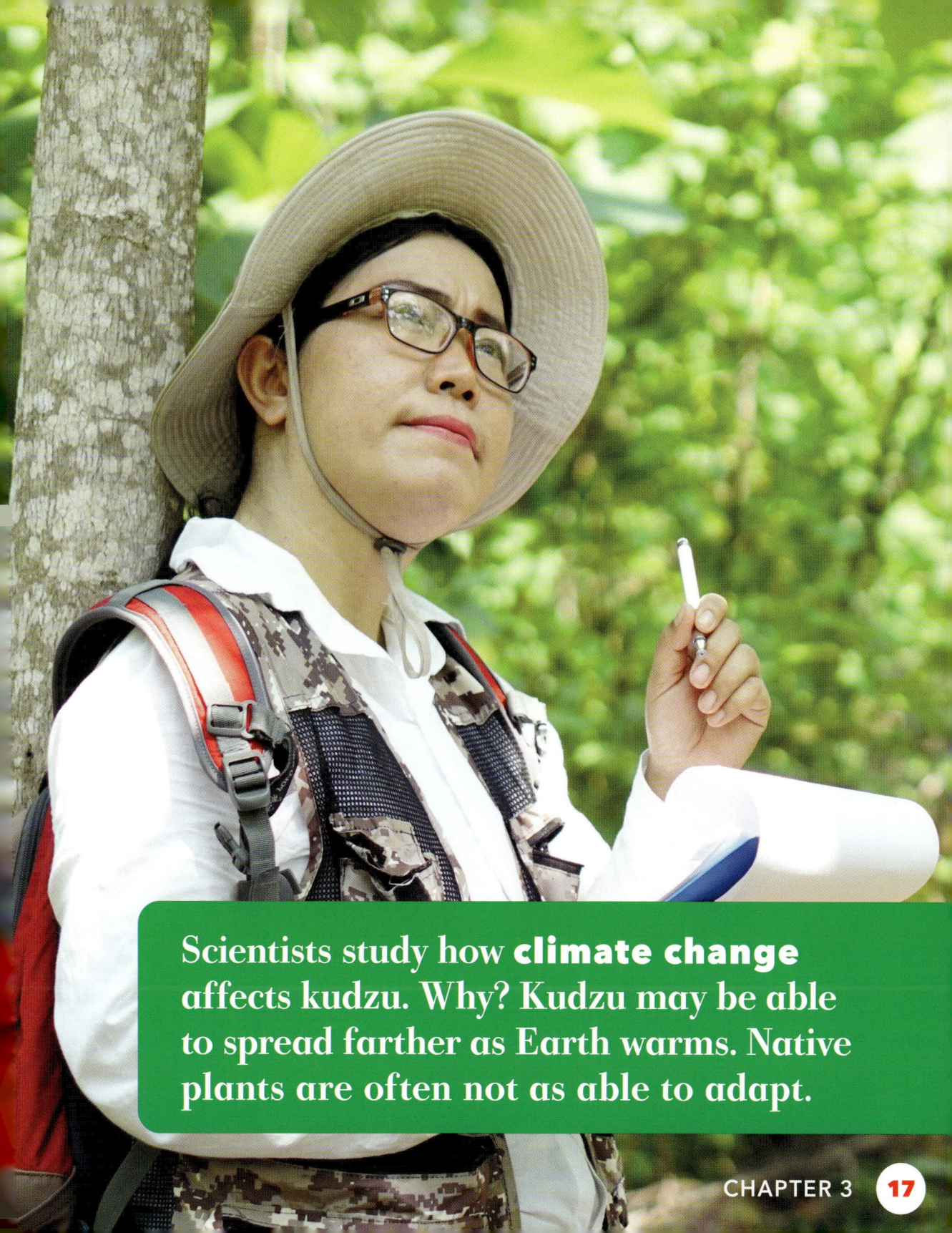

Scientists study how **climate change** affects kudzu. Why? Kudzu may be able to spread farther as Earth warms. Native plants are often not as able to adapt.

People in the United States are trying to stop kudzu from spreading. How? They cut its vines. They pull the plants from the soil. They use chemicals to kill it, too.

DID YOU KNOW?

After removing kudzu, it should be bagged or burned. Why? That way it cannot grow back.

Kudzu is delicious to **livestock**! Cattle and goats eat it. This can help get rid of it. Stopping the spread of kudzu will help native wildlife. How can you help?

ACTIVITIES & TOOLS

GROW A PLANT FROM SEED

Kudzu grows quickly. Grow your own plants from seeds in this fun activity!

What You Need:

- potting soil
- two plastic pots or large mason jars
- two kinds of plant seeds
- water
- pencil
- notebook
- ruler

1. Add potting soil to the pots or mason jars. Fill them about two-thirds full.

2. Make two or three shallow holes at the top of the soil in each pot. Place a seed in each hole. Cover them lightly with soil. Only one type of seed should be in each pot.

3. Water the soil so it is damp.

4. Check the soil every day or two to be sure it doesn't get too dry.

5. Each day, record whether your seeds have sprouted. Once they sprout, use a ruler to measure their growth from the soil to the top of the plant. Write down how big each plant is each day.

6. Kudzu can grow one foot (0.3 m) in a day. How does this compare to the plants you are growing?

GLOSSARY

adapts: Changes to fit a new situation.

biodiversity: The condition of nature in which a wide variety of species live in a single area.

climate change: Changes in Earth's weather and climate over time.

erosion: The wearing away of something by water or wind.

exhibit: An object or collection of objects that are on display.

habitats: The places where animals or plants are usually found.

invasive species: Any kind of living organism that is not native to a specific area.

livestock: Animals that are kept or raised on a farm or ranch.

native: Growing or living naturally in a particular area of the world.

nodes: The parts of a plant stem where leaves come out.

nutrients: Substances such as proteins, minerals, and vitamins that people, animals, and plants need to stay strong and healthy.

pollinate: To take pollen from the male part of a flower and put it on the female part of a flower so the plant can reproduce.

rhizomes: Underground stems of a plant that produce roots below the soil and shoots above it.

runners: Thin, creeping stems that grow out from a plant's base.

vine: A plant that creeps on the ground or climbs with a winding stem.

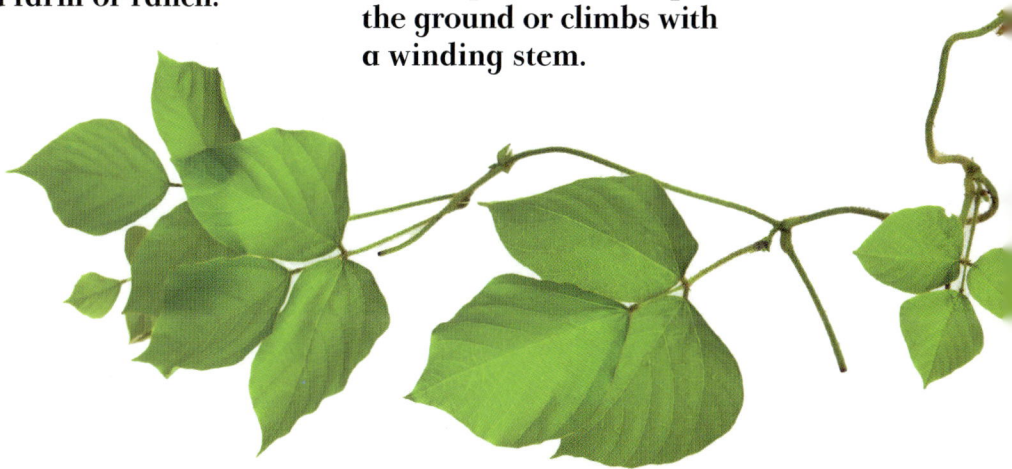

INDEX

TO LEARN MORE

Finding more information is as easy as 1, 2, 3.

1. Go to www.factsurfer.com
2. Enter "kudzu" into the search box.
3. Choose your book to see a list of websites.

FACT SURFER